The big 5
and other wild animals

Lion
Megan Emmett

The big 5 and other wild animals series is published by
Awareness Publishing Group (Pty) Ltd.
Copyright © 2019

Awareness Publishing (SA) (Pty) Ltd
www.awareness.co.za
info@awareness.co.za
+27 (0)86 110 1491
www.facebook.com/AwarenessPublishing

All rights reserved. No part of this publication may be reproduced in any form
without written permission from the publisher, except by a reviewer.

First edition, 2019

Lion by Megan Emmett
ISBN 978-0-6393-0003-0

Summary: An introduction to the lion, one of the Big Five wild animals. This book looks at the lion's family life and territory, its daily activities and its physical characteristics. The book also talks about the conservation of lions.

Book design: Dana Espag and Bianca Keenan-Smith.

Editorial credits: Educational consultant: Gillian Mervis. Copy editor: Danya Ristić. Proofreader: Lynda Gilfillan. Picture editor: Anne Laing. Indexer: Lois C Henderson.

Illustrations: Cartoons: Gerhard Cruywagen of Greenhouse Cartoons, and Dana Espag.
Additional drawings: Dana Espag.

Photo credits: Cover and pp.3 (middle), 6, 8, 9 (top left and right), 10, 11, 26, 27 (middle and right), 30, 32, 34, 36 (top right), 42, 44 (bottom) and 50 © Anne Laing; pp.3 (top), 9 (bottom), 16, 36 (top and bottom left), 39, 40, 44 (top), 45 (middle), 46, 48 (bottom), 51, 52, and 54 © Shem Compion; p.3 (bottom) © Sally Wallis / Shutterstock; p.4 © Denny Allen / Gallo Images; p.7 (top) © Mogens Trolle / Shutterstock pp.7 (bottom), 14 (top), 15, 24, 27 (left), 31, 36 (bottom right), 41, 45 (right) and 48 (top) © Megan Emmett; p.12 © Peter Betts / Shutterstock; p.14 (bottom) © James Harrison / iStockphoto; p.17 © Winfried Wisniewski / Gallo Images; p.18 © Peter Betts / Shutterstock; p.20 © USO / iStockphoto; p.22 © GomezDavid / iStockphoto; p.23 © Peter Betts / Shutterstock; p.28 © Ehlers / iStockphoto; p.35 © Dana Espag; p.38 (top and bottom) © javarman / Shutterstock; p.45 (left) © Dave Pusey / Shutterstock; p.56 © PRILL / Shutterstock.

You can read more by Megan Emmett about animals in the book *Game Ranger in Your Backpack – All-in-one Interpretative Guide to the Lowveld*, published by Briza Publications (2010, Pretoria). ISBN 978-1-920217-06-8.

1 3 5 7 9 0 8 6 4 2

Contents

Quick facts 5
Meet the lion 7
Family life 11
Living in territories 15
Working together 17
Marking a territory 19
Food and water 21
Hunting 23
King of the kill 25
Teeth 27
Roaring 29
Manes 31
Sleeping 33
Claws and tracks 35
Mating 39
Flehmen 41
Giving birth 43
Breeding together 45
"Follow me" signs 47
King of the bush 49
Endangered lions 51
Conservation 53
Glossary 55

Lions are the only cats that live together in big families.

Quick facts

Height (at the shoulder)	Male: 1,2 metres. Female: 1,1 metres
Weight	Male: Generally 190 kilograms, but can be up to 260 kilograms. Female: 130 kilograms
Lifespan	10–14 years (18 at most). Females live longer than males
Gestation (pregnancy)	About 110 days (3,5 months)
Number of young	Generally three, but there can be up to six
Habitat	Many areas, as long as there is grass in which they can **stalk** their prey, and enough medium-sized to large prey
Food	Mainly wildebeest, zebra, impala, waterbuck, warthog, kudu and giraffe, but also a wide range of mammals, from mice to buffalo, and even elephants; birds up to the size of ostriches; snakes and lizards; insects; fish and rotting meat
Predators	Humans, hyenas and other **carnivores**. Pythons kill the cubs
Interesting fact	A lion's skull weighs over three kilograms
Is it one of the Big Five?	Yes!

Words that appear in the text in bold, **like this**, are explained in the Glossary at the end of this book. Some key words are in colour.

A male lion's great strength helps him to hunt big animals.

Meet the lion

Lions are the biggest cats in Africa. Lions are **predators**, which means that they hunt and kill other animals. They are extremely powerful and can hunt large animals such as antelope, or buck, and buffalo.

Lions are part of a group of animals that we call the Big Five. These are the biggest and most dangerous animals in the wild. The other animals in the Big Five group are buffalo, elephant, rhino and leopard. Long ago, people from Europe used to come to Africa to hunt the Big Five to show that they were brave. Nowadays, many people go on holiday to a game reserve to see the Big Five.

Lions live in family groups, or prides. They are the only cats that do this. Other cats, such as leopards, live alone. Every lion pride lives and hunts in a specific area, or territory. Lions do not allow other prides to come into their territory.

Lion cubs like to spend time playing with each other.

A male and female lion watch out for prey to hunt.

Like all cats, lions lick themselves and each other clean.

Meet the lion continued

All the lions in a pride hunt together, but it is mainly the females that do the hunting. They work together to kill **prey** that is big enough to feed the whole family. But they are not always successful. Often their prey gets away, and they do not manage to catch and kill it.

Living in a pride is also good when lions have cubs, because they can all help to care for the young.

Lions are the biggest cats in Africa.

Male lions rule over the pride.

Family life

Female lions are called lionesses. All the lionesses in a pride are related – they are either sisters, or mothers and daughters. They stay together their whole lives. But if a family becomes too large, the lionesses divide into two smaller prides. They still live in the same territory, and meet up from time to time.

A few big males rule over the pride. They protect their pride and keep all other males away. They even chase their own sons away when they are about three years old, which is when the younger lions are nearly old enough to mate.

Lion cubs grow up together in a pride. Male cubs then get chased away by the ruling males once they are old enough to live on their own.

After a young male lion has left the pride, he moves from place to place until he grows big enough to fight for his own territory.

Family life continued

Young male lions are too small to have their own territories. They are only big enough to fight for a territory when they are about five years old. In the meantime, after the older lions have chased them away, they become **nomadic** and move from place to place. If older lions catch young males sneaking through their territories, they chase the young males away. Male lions are fully grown at seven years.

Young, strong males sometimes take the territories of old males. Then the old males leave, and become nomadic. They usually die when they are about ten years old, because they are killed by other lions. They may also starve to death, as they find it difficult to hunt on their own and they do not have any females to hunt for them.

Male lions protect the territory where the pride lives.

Lions drink water often. They need to have a source of water in their territory.

Living in territories

A good territory needs three things: water for the lions to drink, lots of animals for them to hunt, and bushes with shade where they can rest. Lions also need bushes to hide behind when they hunt.

A pride of lions keeps all other lions out of its territory. Sometimes a single male will protect the pride, but more often a few males work together to protect a big territory.

Females also have territories. Their territories are smaller than those of the males. The females take part of a male's territory as their own, and do not allow other females to enter their territory.

Male lions chase away other lions, including females, if they are not part of their pride.

In a group called a coalition, male lions work together to protect a territory.

Working together

When male lions work together to protect their territory, we call them a **coalition**. There can be two to five males in a coalition, and often they are brothers.

These males do not stay together all the time. They often split up to guard different parts of the territory. If they need to, they can find each other again quickly.

Working as a team has more rewards than working alone. It is easier for a few younger lions to chase an older male away when they try to take over the older lion's territory.

Hyenas are the lions' biggest enemy, and a team works well together to keep hyenas away. Together, the males can protect a bigger area, and they can also have more lioness prides to mate with and to do their hunting for them.

Hyenas hang around lions at a kill, waiting for their chance to feed.

A lion rubs the smell from his cheeks onto a plant to mark his territory.

Marking a territory

Lions spend a lot of time marking their territory. This lets other lions know where the territory begins and ends. Lions mark by roaring and by scent-marking. A lion scent-marks when it leaves behind smells from its urine and dung.

Lions spray urine backwards onto bushes and rocks. They also **defecate**, leaving their **dung**, or waste matter, in open areas. After urinating or defecating, they scrape the area with their paws. The smell gets on their paws, and as they walk they leave that smell behind on the ground.

Lions also give off a smell from their cheeks. To leave this smell behind, they rub their faces on plants as they walk, marking their territories.

Lions do not like to fight with each other, in case they get hurt. They need to stay well and strong so that they can protect their pride and hunt for food. This is another reason why lions mark their territories – to keep away from each other.

A lioness with a newborn antelope that she has killed.

Food and water

Lions eat any animals that are available. They mostly hunt antelope, but will eat almost anything, from a mouse to an elephant. They also eat old, rotten meat, called **carrion**.

Lions find food in various ways: they can be scavengers, stealing the food of other predators. They often hide at waterholes to attack animals that come to drink. Sometimes, they dig warthogs out of the warthogs' holes, or catch baby antelope that are hiding in the grass. Lions also play an important role in the wild because they kill off sick and weak animals. By killing sick animals, lions help other animals to stay healthy, because a sick animal can make other animals sick too.

Lions hunt mostly at night, but they also hunt during the day if they have the chance. When they have killed their prey, they eat as much as they can in case they do not get the chance to kill another animal again soon. Sometimes, when they have finished eating, the lions are so fat that they can hardly move! But the food digests and breaks down in their stomachs quickly, so that they can eat again soon.

Like most cats, lions have rough tongues. They can actually remove meat from the bone just by licking it. The juice from the meat gives lions most of the liquid that they need to survive, but they still drink often if water is available.

A lioness holds a zebra by the throat until it dies from lack of air to breathe.

Hunting

When a predator sneaks or creeps up on its prey, we say that it is stalking. Leopards are the best stalkers of all the cats, but lions are also very good at stalking. A lion can even stalk where there is not much bush to hide behind. Keeping its head and body close to the ground, the lion sneaks up on its prey slowly and carefully. It watches its prey, and if the prey looks up, the lion freezes on the spot, standing completely still.

A lioness stalking her prey.

If the prey sees the lion, it will try to run away. The lion will chase it, but only for a short way. Lions can run 100 metres in six seconds at top speed, but not for long, because they become tired easily.

Lions usually attack the animal's shoulders or rump, just near the tail. A lion is extremely heavy and the weight of its body makes the prey fall down. It then grabs the prey by the throat or by the nose, and the prey suffocates – it dies because it cannot breathe.

Male lions eat first. But if the kill is big, the males let the females eat at the same time.

King of the kill

Lionesses do most of the hunting. The males help the females when they attack large animals such as giraffe and buffalo. Males can also hunt alone.

Males always eat first. Sometimes they take over the whole kill, and leave only a small portion for the lionesses and cubs. The lionesses let the males do this because the males are bigger and stronger than they are. It is also a reward for the males, because they protect the females from hyenas and other male lions.

Male lions that are not part of a pride are a threat, as they may harm the pride. If they take over a territory, they kill all the cubs that are less than one year old. This is because if a lioness's cubs have been killed, she becomes ready to mate again. The new males then mate with the lionesses so that they can have their own cubs while they are still in charge of the pride.

Females do not fall pregnant straight away. They wait for the new males to prove that they are the strongest. Sometimes, the new males are chased away by other new males, and the females do not want to lose their cubs all over again.

A lion yawns, showing his long, sharp canine and carnassial teeth.

Teeth

An animal that eats other animals is a carnivore. Lions are the largest carnivores in Africa. But not all carnivores hunt. Some carnivores, such as the aardwolf, eat insects.

All carnivores have the same kinds of teeth. They have special teeth on the sides of their mouths, which help them to chew meat off the bone. These teeth are called carnassials (car-NA-see-als). The carnassials are thin and sharp, and they work like the blades of a pair of scissors to cut the meat. When an animal chews with these teeth, we say that it is gnawing its food.

The lion has long, sharp teeth at the front of its mouth. These are the canines. Canines help the lion to grip and kill its prey. These teeth are used only for killing, not for eating. Lions have powerful lower jaws so that they can hold on to their prey. They also have strong muscles on their large skulls, or heads.

Lions roar to tell other lions where they are and where their territories begin and end.

Roaring

Some cats in the wild can roar. They use their larynx (LA-rinks), or voice box, to roar. When air moves from the lungs through the larynx out of the mouth, the larynx vibrates, or moves quickly back and forth. This vibration creates the roaring sound. A chain of small bones holds and supports the larynx inside a wild cat's throat. In some cats, this small-bone chain is solid and cannot bend, so the sounds that these cats make are not very loud. But in a group of cats called *Panthera*, the small-bone chain is loose, and it can bend. Along with leopards, lions belong to the *Panthera* group. And because the chain of small bones in *Panthera* cats can bend, the larynx can vibrate more easily and these cats can roar very loudly.

Lions roar to let other lions know where their territory is. They also roar when they need to find other lions from their pride.

Lions roar mostly at night, when they are active. At night, when the air is still, sound travels further. Sometimes a lion's roar can be heard from as far as seven kilometres away. Lions know each other's roars and are able to answer them.

Lions also moan, purr, growl and snarl, and the cubs meow.

An adult male lion, with the long, thick hair on his neck and shoulders that is his mane.

Manes

An adult male lion has thick, longer hair over his neck and shoulders. We call this his mane. A mane makes him look big and scary to other males. It also makes lionesses want to mate with him.

The mane protects the lion when he is fighting. When male lions fight, they face each other head-to-head. They try to scratch each other with their long, sharp claws. These claws can cause deep and painful wounds.

It takes a long time for a lion's mane to grow. His mane is usually fully grown by the time he is seven years old. The size and thickness of the lion's mane helps to show how old he is. Younger males have a small amount of hair, and this hair sticks up between their ears.

Lionesses usually mate only with males that have fully grown manes. The size and colour of a male's mane helps the female to choose a mate.

A young male lion's mane sticks up on his head, between his ears.

A lion sleeping on his back.

Sleeping

Lions spend most of their time lying around and sleeping. They sleep or rest for about 20 hours of each day! This is because they use a lot of energy when they hunt. They put almost all their energy into catching their prey. Looking after the territory also uses up energy, because the lions often have to walk a long way.

Lions may seem to be fast asleep at times, but they are still **alert**. This means that they can be on their feet in a second, ready to attack.

When they wake up in the evening, lions in a pride enjoy their time together as a family. We call this **social** behaviour. They yawn, lick each other, defecate, urinate and roar together. All this helps to create teamwork in the pride.

Even lion cubs have big, sharp claws.

Claws and tracks

Lions have large, sharp claws. They use their claws to fight and hunt. When the claws are at rest and not in use, they remain hidden in the paws in special little cases called **sheaths**. These sheaths protect the claws and stop them from becoming blunt while the lion walks around. When lions need these claws, they use certain muscles to push the claws out. Later, when these muscles are relaxed again, the claws spring back into their sheaths.

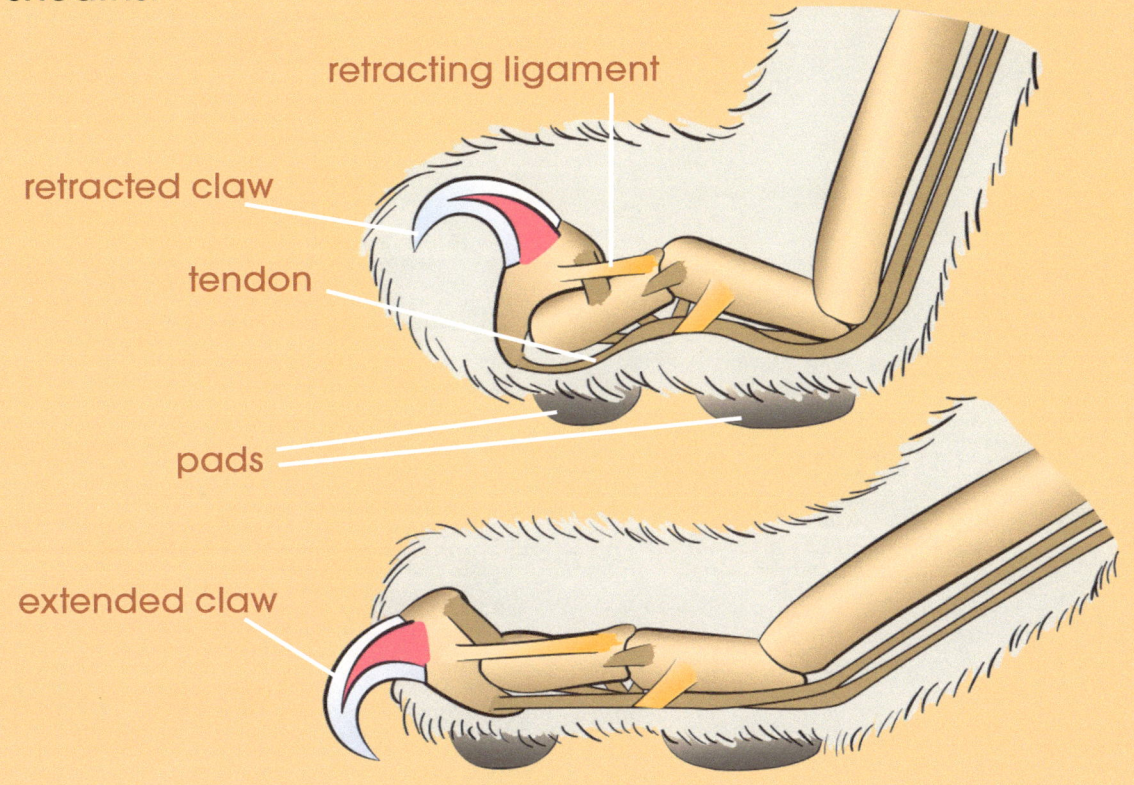

Top: A lion's claw is retracted or hidden inside the paw when not in use.
Bottom: A lion's claw is extended or pushed out of the paw when it is being used. The tendon and ligament help the claw to move in and out of the paw.

A lion's back paw. Lions have cushions on their paws called pads.

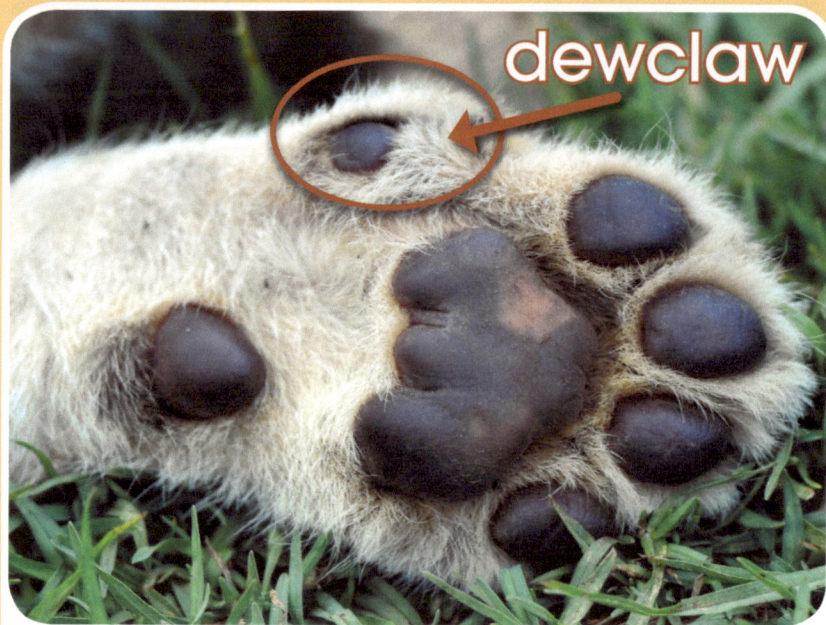

A lion's front paw. The pads on a lion's paws help the lion to walk quietly.

A lion's footprint, or track, is the biggest of all the cats and other predators.

A lion's track, showing four toes in front and three bumps at the back.

Claws and tracks continued

Lions also have an extra, small claw on their front paws. This is called the dewclaw. It is higher up at the back of their front paws. The dewclaw helps a lion to grip prey and to climb trees.

Lions have the largest tracks, or footprints, of all the cats. One footprint is 13 to 15 centimetres long. Soft pads underneath the paw help a lion to walk quietly, so that it can catch its prey. There is one big pad and four smaller toe pads. A lion's big pad has three bumps at the back, while a hyena's pad has two bumps. So the number of bumps at the back of the footprint, three or two, shows if it is a lion or a hyena that has been in the area.

Leopard tracks look like lion tracks, but leopard tracks are smaller – about 9 to 10 centimetres long. Leopard tracks are also rounder than lion tracks.

While they are mating, a pair of lions will stay together for four days and nights, doing almost nothing else.

A male lion and lioness mating.

Mating

Lionesses do not fall pregnant easily. When a lioness is ready for mating, we say that she is in heat or in **oestrus** (EE-striss). A female and a male have to mate many times for the lioness to become pregnant. A lion pair will mate every 20 minutes, for four days and nights. Each time lions mate, it takes about one minute.

A lioness turns around to swat the male after they have mated.

Lions mate over a long time for two reasons. First, it helps the female to release eggs in her body, and this helps her to fall pregnant. For every cub that reaches one year of age, the mother lioness will have mated 3 000 times! Second, the long mating confuses the males as to which one is the father. The male that begins mating with a female may become extremely tired by day three or four. If he does, another of the coalition males will take over. Each of the males then thinks that the cubs are his, so both will protect the cubs when they are born.

The male bites the female's neck during mating. He also snarls, growling loudly and baring his teeth. When the pair has finished mating the male withdraws his penis. This is often painful for the female, and she turns around and swats, or slaps, him with her paw.

*Male lions make funny faces when they do flehmen.
By doing flehmen, the male finds out if a female is ready to mate.*

Flehmen

A male can tell if a female is in oestrus by doing flehmen (FLE-men). Flehmen is a way by which some animals use the top of their mouth to detect and discover smells left by other animals. The word comes from the German word *flehmen*, which means "curling up the upper lip".

The male does flehmen by sniffing the rump or behind of a female, or by sniffing the ground where she has urinated. He then pulls back his top lip and makes a frown. When he lifts his lip, a small hole or gland on the roof of his mouth opens. The gland picks up chemicals in the female's urine. These chemicals tell the male if the female is ready to mate or not.

A male lion doing flehmen.

A lion cub rubs against its mother. While the cubs are small and still need to be hidden away, the lioness visits them to feed them.

Giving birth

The length of time that a female is pregnant is the **gestation** period. Although lions are big animals, a lioness is pregnant for only 3,5 months. This is because, to eat, a lioness needs to hunt, and it is difficult for her to hunt with a heavy belly. So the gestation period is short.

Because lionesses have a short gestation, their cubs are not well developed when they are born. The cubs' eyes are closed, and they are helpless. The helpless cubs need to be kept safe for six weeks after birth, so the lioness hides them in a cave or in thick bush. During this time, they grow and become stronger until they are ready for their mother to take them to meet the rest of the pride.

Animals that do not have to hunt have much longer gestation periods, and so their young are born much more developed. **Antelope**, for example, only need to eat grass to survive. So having a big belly during her pregnancy does not stop the female antelope from eating. But once baby antelope are born, they must be developed enough to be able to run away from predators. Therefore an antelope's gestation period is much longer than a lioness's. The young antelope are born with their eyes open, and they can move around soon after birth.

Lion cubs drink milk from their mothers or from any other female in the pride that has cubs.

Lion cubs sometimes have to push each other out of the way to get to the mother's teats and drink her milk.

Breeding together

The lionesses in a pride often come into heat at the same time. They also fall pregnant, and have their cubs, at the same time. This helps the pride, because the mothers can then care for each other's cubs.

The cubs survive on milk from their mothers. If some of the lionesses need to be away from their babies to hunt, another mother can feed or **suckle** the cubs, giving them milk from her teats.

Sometimes, cubs stay hidden from the pride for longer than six weeks. This happens when there are already older cubs in the pride. Older cubs are bigger and stronger than the babies, and they are able to get to the mother's teats more easily than the little cubs. The older cubs would drink all the milk and the younger cubs would starve if the mother did not keep them separate from the pride.

When the pride moves, their black tail-tips and the black fur behind their ears help them to stay together. These markings are especially useful when the lions are walking through long grass.

"Follow me" signs

All cats use their tails and ears to show how they are feeling.

Lions have long tails with a small bunch of black hair on the end. They also have black fur behind their ears. These are "follow me" signs. They are important for the pride for two main reasons.

First, when cubs walk with their mother in long grass, the black tip of her tail is easy to follow because it is at the correct height for them to see it. The cubs also use the black tip as a target when they practise **pouncing**, or jumping.

Second, the black tail is used as a sign when lions hunt. From behind, the lions can all see each other's black ears and black tail-tips. There is no black to be seen from the front, and so their prey do not notice them. Lions watch each other when they hunt. The twitch of an ear or a flick of the tail helps the lions to know what another lion is going to do next.

A black-backed jackal feeds on a buffalo killed by lions.

A lion taking the remains of a young zebra that was killed by another predator. This is called scavenging.

King of the bush

Lions are the biggest and strongest predators in the wild. So when they meet other predators, lions are **dominant**. We call lions super-predators. They **scavenge**, stealing food from other predators, and they even kill other predators' babies. They also kill smaller carnivores for food.

The only real enemies of lions are hyenas. But even then, hyenas are only a threat to lions when there are many hyenas together, in a clan. Even a whole clan of hyenas will not win a fight with a pride of lions if the male lions are there. But sometimes, elephants and herds of buffalo chase and even kill lions in order to protect their young.

Hyenas, jackals and vultures visit the kills that lions make and try to steal the leftovers.

White lions

*Some lions are completely white. These lions are rare – there are about 500 of them in the world. Usually, white lions can only be seen in a zoo, but there are also some in a game reserve called Timbavati next to the Kruger Park. Lions' coats are white if they have too little of the **melanin** pigment, or colouring matter, in their fur. Two normal-coloured lions can have a white cub.*

Endangered lions

Lions live mainly in Africa. A few live in India. Long ago, lions also lived in Europe and Asia. Nowadays we find them mostly in eastern and southern Africa, in game reserves or in protected areas.

There are lions in countries such as South Africa, Botswana, Namibia, Zimbabwe and Mozambique. Scientists think that there are only about 25 000 lions left in the world. Many years ago there were hundreds of thousands of lions!

Lions have become endangered.

There are hardly any animals left for lions to kill and eat, outside game reserves. Many cities, towns, villages and farms have been built in Africa, and these have taken up the areas where lions and their prey used to live. Also, when lions escape from a game reserve, people chase them away and even kill them. This is because people are scared of lions, and because lions kill farmers' sheep and cows.

Because most lions live only in protected areas these days, we say that they are endangered. There is a chance that they may become extinct, or die off completely.

Researchers often put radio collars on wild lions. These collars make a beep sound on the researchers' radio, and this helps them to find the lions, so that they can learn more about them.

Conservation

To conserve wildlife, we protect wild animals and the places where these animals live. There are three ways that people help to conserve lions:

First, by setting up game reserves. Game reserves are large areas of open space where lions can live and hunt their prey. Many game reserves have electric fences around them. This keeps the lions and their prey inside the game reserve safe, because people cannot harm them there. People living next to the game reserves are also safe, as lions cannot harm them. But having fences around game reserves does mean that the lions are no longer free to move from one place to another.

Second, by studying lions' **habits** and the way they live. We call this research. Researchers look at how lions hunt, what lions eat and how they decide on their territories. By learning more about lions, people can make sure that game reserves are large enough for lions to live safely and stay healthy.

Third, by educating people in nearby areas. People who work in conservation are called conservationists. They teach the communities living in areas around game reserves about lions. Conservationists teach farmers how to keep their sheep and cows safe from lions, and what to do if a lion attacks their animals. If farmers know what to do when a lion comes onto their farms, they will not shoot it.

These two lions could well be brothers, as the male lions in a coalition are usually related to each other.

Glossary

alert - quick to notice and react to danger

antelope - any animal with pointed horns that looks something like a deer; also called a buck

carnivore - an animal that eats other animals

carrion - the rotting flesh of a dead animal

coalition - a group of male lions that work together to protect a territory

defecate - to produce dung from the body

dominant - bigger and stronger

dung - an animal's solid waste matter

gestation - the time that a female is pregnant

habits - the things that people and animals repeat, or do again and again

melanin - the pigment, or colouring matter, that makes an animal's fur a certain colour, either just in places or all over

nomadic - moving from place to place

oestrus - the times when a female is ready to mate

Like leopards, lions can climb up trees. But lions are heavy, so they do not climb trees often because it is difficult for them to do.

Glossary continued

pouncing – jumping quickly on something to catch it

predators – animals that hunt and kill other animals for food

prey – an animal that is hunted and killed by another animal for food

scavenge – to steal food from another animal

sheaths – close-fitting, protective covers for things, such as claws, that can be drawn and pulled out of the covers

social – spending time together as a family and as a pride

stalk – to sneak or creep up on prey

suckle – to drink milk from a mother's teats

suffocates – dies because of being unable to breathe

territory – the specific area where only one animal, or group of animals, lives

tracks – an animal's footprints

www.ingramcontent.com/pod-product-compliance
Lightning Source LLC
Chambersburg PA
CBHW041322290426

44108CB00004B/105